GW00390843

_ife and Death in the Prehistoric North

A SELECTION OF SITES
IN CUMBRIA AND NORTHUMBERLAND

Stan Beckensall, BA, Dip Ed, FSA (Scot), FSA

First published in Great Britain in 1994
by Butler Publishing
Thropton, Morpeth, Northumberland NE65 7LP

ISBN 0 946928 45 2

·inted by Mayfair Printers Ltd., Print House, Commercial Rd., Hendon, Sunderland SR2 8NP

"**Prehistory**" refers to the time before written evidence, which in Cumbria a Northumberland means before the Romans took over.

"**Archaeology**" is the process that uncovers part of the picture of life, throu observation in the field and through excavation.

LANDSCAPE

Prehistory pieces together ways in which people adapted to, and changed, the landscape in order to live.

The basic rock structures, soils and rivers were there to be used, avoided, or crossed. The land was covered with grass, trees, flowers and mosses and inhabited by birds and animals, but it has changed since people began to use it. There is no such thing as a 'natural' landscape, for all that we see today has been changed in some way. There have been variations in climate, but the principal cause is human activity. At no time is this more obvious than at present.

Some land is not suitable tor living on: the mountains of the Lake District or the high Pennines, for example. But rare quality rock, however high up, could be turned into axes that were so good that people all over the country wanted to be thought important by owning one. So despite the cold, the wet and other hazards, a group of people over 5,000 years ago specialized in making them at Langdale. This was exceptional, though. People were farmers and herdsmen and growing food or keeping animals demanded low slopes, valleys and rich vegetation growing on good soils.

Our starting point, therefore, should be where people farmed. Non-farmers existed thousands of years before that, leaving minute traces on the landscape of their hunting and gathering activities, but what can be seen today begins with the greatest revolution in history: the gradual introduction of crops, that fre people from total dependence animals, fish and wild vegetation.

People did continue to wander, a animals of all kinds were vital to th economy, but once cereals we grown, parts of the landscape becar places of settlement and places whe all the scattered people could gath together periodically to trade, ch make marriage contracts, worship a feel that they were part of a commun In any such grouping there were tho who had more strength, wealth a influence and would come out on tc A liking for luxury and personal van are not new: some had necklaces a other ornaments, superior pottery a weapons. Power takes many form but the display of riches, as with toda bigger home or car, was popular. T root of all power, though, was yc ability to use the landscape not only survive, but to produce a surplus th you could bargain and trade with, with which you could buy allegiance

Mountains, hills, fells, valleys, coas plains, volcanic rock, sandstones of ma colours, textures and degrees hardness, limestone, coal, shale a liberal deposits of soils and clays broug down by glacier and river all create t landscape that we see today. But it what happens to the immediate cov that is important to life. The chang brought about in prehistoric times we great. Almost all our present field syster may have been in use, hacked and bu from great tracts of forest. Again, at time when we witness the destructi

the world's forests today, it is a
miliar process. Because the best land
s been farmed over and over again,
s almost eliminates traces of past
riculture, but there are survivals.
imate changes slowly and places
come warmer, colder, wetter or drier.
nd, especially thin soils, loses fertility
being overworked, and grass,
ather and bracken take over. Even
en, marginal lands are re-used and
andoned again. Today farmers are
id not to grow anything in some
lds.

HE EVIDENCE

ere may be nothing to see of these
cient fields at ground level: that's where
bird's eye view is so useful. Ditches,
ugh scars, old beaten tracks and roads
ntinue to show up thousands of years
er where the modern plough has not
ite reached. We are given examples,
rough air photographs, field-walking
d excavations from which we build up
artial picture.

ience has come to the aid of
chaeologists. Grains of pollen, sealed
can be identified and counted in
cient soils. The plants that they reveal
n tell us about the conditions in which
ey grow best. Snails flourish in special
nditions. Carbon remains can be
ted. Interred bones and cremations
ve their story to tell as do pots,
plements of daily life, weapons and the
mains of dwellings and defences. Like
, people lost things, broke them and
ew them away. They didn't have much,
t like our well-filled dustbins and landfill
es, but there is enough to give us some
a of their lives. Stone age technology
pended largely on flint: nodules that
uld be smashed up and worked into
ades, axes, arrows, scrapers, awls,

borers and saws. There we have part of
the story: animals were killed, gutted,
skinned, the meat eaten, skin scraped out
and processed and sewn together to
make clothes, tents and carriers.

Flint does not rot, but organic materials
decay. The survival of wood, cloth and
skins is a happy coincidence, where the
decay process has been arrested. Bodies
in the bog are rare, extreme examples of
this process.

MUSEUMS

To find evidence that has been removed
from its original location, through
excavation, accidental find, or field-
walking, you may go to museums.
Carlisle, Penrith, Newcastle and Berwick
hold enough of the prehistoric past to give
a good idea of changing fashions in stone
and metal artefacts, ornaments and
pottery. There, the objects will have been
classified into periods of time and types.
Some archaeologists spend much of their
lives making complex classifications of
such objects, making accurate records
and relating them to the context in which
they were found.

TIME SCALES

"**Stone age**" covers so many thousands
of years that it's not a very helpful
category, but it's based mainly on the use
of stone to make weapons, digging tools
and tools that process animals and make
things from them.

'Lithos' is a Greek word that means stone.
The "Stone ages" are named palaeo-,
meaning old-lithic, meso-middle-lithic
and neo-new-lithic.

When copper, tin, bronze and gold
appear, historians mark the change by
calling it the **Bronze Age**. After that it's
the **Iron Age.**

3

This doesn't mean that someone shouts, "All change!" and flint gives way
bronze, or bronze to iron. Metals were rare, their manufacture a special sk
and probably only affordable by a few. Flint in most parts of our region is n
indigenous, had to be imported, and it carried on being used long after met
was introduced. However, the passing of time is marked by the way in whic
some technology developed, traceable in the changing shapes of tools a
weapons. If such things can be dated by being found in a definite context whic
itself is datable, this provides a time-scale so that an object, for example, foun
in plough soil can be dated. So all this work of classification is important
dating thousands of objects, but when it comes to flint, there are many piece
struck off in manufacture that cannot be dated.

A selection of sites has been made, which will be described and fitted into
time-scale. There may be no good example of a particular type of monument
the region, in which case you may have to look further afield.

NEOLITHIC MONUMENTS (c.4,300 - 2,100BC)

People who live by hunting and gathering move about a lot, but don't lea
much trace of their lives.

A great revolution took place in agriculture, which led to surplus food suppli
and an increase in population. It freed some energy from mere food-gatherin
and specialised attention was paid to monument-building, pottery-making a
the manufacture of fine tools and weapons from flint and other stones - notab
Langdale stone. It was a time when much of our present arable farming are
were cleared and cultivated, and many of these field systems have bee
discovered from the air. Monuments that can be seen from the ground are mo
obvious.

MAYBURGH HENGE STONE AND ENTRANCE . EAMONT BRIDGE IN THE BACKGROUN
The centre is 87m (287') in diameter, with a 36m (120') wide bank, 4m (14') high. The stone, all th
remains of a circle that was blown up, is 3m (9') high. The entrance gap had four stones flanking
Only 13 out of 78 British henges have stone circles inside; others may have had stone settings

4

ENGES

hereas Northumberland's known henges are buried on the Milfield Plain tween Wooler and Coldstream, two of the finest upstanding henges are near :nrith.

fit these henges into a time scale, it is useful to note that Stonehenge's first ase was a low wall made from the upcast of a shallow circular ditch in about 100BC, the big sarcens were erected in 2,000BC, and its final phase was 300BC. It is also wise to note that, despite the many books that have been itten about that famous monument, we still know little about it.

ayburgh (NY 519 285) is a henge that is made of a huge wall of stones closing a circular area, with a gap allowing an entrance. Inside is a single inding stone, but at one time there were more in the centre and at the trance. To make the wall, millions of rounded stones were brought in from e surrounding fields and River Eamont. There is no ditch around this henge.

ng Arthur's Round Table (NY 523 284) is quite different in style from ayburgh: a circular ditch interrupted by two 'causewayed' entrances (i.e. the ound has been left undug there to form a bridge). The upcast from the digging the ditch was heaped around outside the ditch to form a bank. It is still pressive, even though a road cuts the north part off, and in the last century a a garden was built on it. Part of the wall that surrounded the henge has been ttened in recent times to make a platform for a building. Also recent is a faint t mound spread in the centre; there have been reports of cremations buried ere.

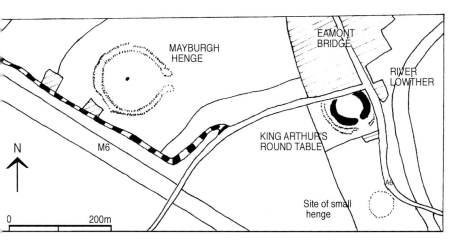

As there has been no recent scientific excavation at either of these sites, they can only be partially understood by referring to what is generally known about henges.

It is possible that they may have had a circular arrangement of wooden posts inside, which in turn may have been replaced with standing stones which, as we know at Mayburgh, were taken out in modern times.

Much has been written about astronomical alignments of stones and posts within henges. It is understandable that a farming community should want to mark changes in the position of sun and moon, for their life was governed by the seasons.

Considerable time and labour was used to make them. King Arthur's site has a large ditch that was probably dug with tools as basic as wedges made from deer antlers and shovels made of oxen shoulder blades, and the material moved with the help of woven baskets to build the wall. Mayburgh involved manual shifting of millions of rocks to build the wall and the erection of large standing stones.

All this effort, but who made it, and why? Some guesswork and some reasonable assumptions: the people who made these henges would have farmed the area for miles around, and henges were focal points of other kinds of activity. Construction would have been a communal project. Either there was a strong motive that made so many contribute to such a monument that had a ceremonial use, or people were forced into building it.

Whilst it is unlikely that the age wa one of peace and unity in the servic of the Earth Mother, as some wou like us to believe, it is also unlikely th populations would be coerced in building hundreds of monuments a over Britain. There were more tha we can see today, including sma versions rather like the equivalent parish churches, whilst Mayburg was more like a cathedral.

Someone must have been directir the labour force, setting out a site to basic pattern. Perhaps there was a element of keeping up with th Joneses, or a local pride. There wa a third, destroyed when a ne approach to Lowther Park lodge gate was made in 1878. To construct thre so close together must have been a impressive display of power, but w don't know what relationship they ha to one another. As for their use, the must have been meeting places for a sorts of purposes, including religiou practices that sometimes involved th deposit of burnt bones, although the are not cemeteries. In bringir together scattered people, they wou be places to catch up with the new to exchange goods and perhaps arrange the equivalent of marriag contracts. They were bigger tha anything else in the locality, just a medieval churches were bigger tha people's houses.

THE EARLY BRONZE AGE
(c.2,100BC)

The Early Bronze Age is one of thos transitional periods that can k confusing because historians are n sure what to put in it. All that can k said definitely is that metal begins ke an appearance. It's useful to think again of a site like Stonehenge nning from about 3,100BC to 1,400BC, beginning with a henge, an avenue de between 2,300-1,700BC, the first erection of the huge sarcen stones in 00BC, and the change of plan in 1,800BC, after which the region continues e used for elaborate burial. Avebury was in decline in 1,900BC.

Early Bronze Age thus includes the building of most of what you see at nehenge today including the numerous bumps in fields, which are the ains of largely single-grave burials.

hange in burial customs is a useful guide to the transition, because we have usands of "round barrows" all over our region. We also have a change from ges to stone circles, and a type of burial that combines the stone circle and n, known as a "ring cairn".

ny sites do not fall neatly into one period; so what follows must be read with t in mind.

JG ARTHUR'S ROUND TABLE

e causewayed entrance crosses the ditch from the left. The trees, top left, stand on the Mayburgh nge.

STONE CIRCLES

Cumbria has many good stone circles, the best to visit being "Long Meg and her Daughters" and Castlerigg.

Although there is surprisingly little known about them, there is plenty to see, and the places where they are set are exciting. Places of special importance to prehistoric people were chosen for reasons that we may not understand. A more obvious reason to choose a place is that it can be seen from a distance, or that much can be seen from it. As soon as we begin to 'feel' things about sites, we have to be careful what we are projecting into them.

Long Meg and her Daughters
(NY 571 372)

The site has free access, easily reached by minor road, 5 miles from Penrith, 2 miles north of Langwathby.

Names were given to stone circles long after the sites were built or used. They were so awe-inspiring that people thought of them as the work of something supernatural. It is common in folklore for evil creatures, creatures of darkness, to be caught in the light and turned to stone, as punishment. It is easy to see how 'Long Meg' could be thought of as a petrified witch. This large pillar of red sandstone was mounted outside the circle, by an entrance, and can be seen as a creature with a pointed head or cap. Her children, her daughters, are made of a different material, boulders of volcanic porphyrite. The difference between

Long Meg and her daughters is n only in the type of stone, but in th varied motifs that have been pecke into the rock. We do not know wh the relationship is in time between th monolith and the circle.

The circle is only part of a lar ceremonial complex, the extent which has been revealed by infra r air photographs. It is flattened to th north where it meets an earlier lar ditched enclosure, invisible from th ground.

There was a smaller circle of ston nearby, seen in 1725, and two oth buried enclosures.

We know that there were bur mounds in the centre, possibly add later. The 'portal' entrance in th south-west, marked by two ext stones, is aligned from the centre the point of the mid-winter sunset.

Two other important sites, Glasson and Little Meg, are part of the rit complex in which ditched enclosure standing stones and burial moun played their part and may have be used for centuries.

LONG MEG OUTSIDE THE PORTAL ENTRANCE OF THE STONE CIRCLE

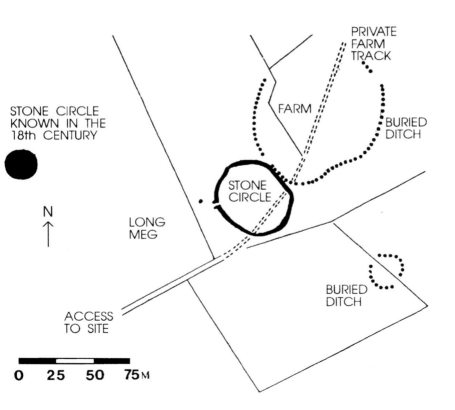

PRIVATE
FARM
TRACK

STONE CIRCLE
KNOWN IN THE
18th CENTURY

FARM

BURIED
DITCH

N

STONE
CIRCLE

LONG
MEG

BURIED
DITCH

ACCESS
TO SITE

0   25   50   75 M

LONG MEG: THE SYMBOLS ON A
SURFACE THAT HAS BEEN OFTEN USED.

Photogragh by Paul Frodsha

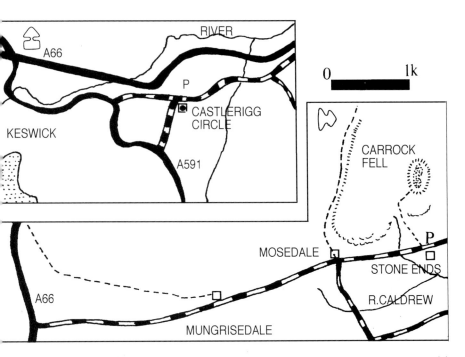

Castlerigg (NY 292 236)

1¹/₂ miles east of Keswick, this is one of the most-visited stone circles. It has very dramatic sweep of scenery as its setting and many of the original 42 stone are still standing. It is known as 'The Carles' -men turned into stone for wrong doing. Two tall stones mark a northern entrance, and despite rig and furrow ploughing, there are traces of a bank around the circle. One peculiar feature a unique box-like arrangement of stones attached to the east stones. There at reports of cairns inside the circle, but the centre has been very disturbed.

Although it is such a spectacular circle, little is known about it.

CASTLERIGG - the unique box-like addition inside the circle.

Duddo (NT 931 437)

Northumberland has few stone circles, although one of the most attractive is small one on private land at Duddo ('Dudda's ridge'). Permission to visit mus be sought from Duddo Farm. The stones were selected for their shapes; natura erosion has resulted in fluting and large cup marks, although there are fou artificially made cup marks on the outer face of one stone.

There is no definite evidence of what the circle was for, but it is situated in suc a way that it commands wide views across the Cheviots and over the Scottis Border.

THE DUDDO STONE

TANDING STONES

utside stone circles, there are isolated stones or alignments of standing ones, some of which are all that remain of bigger features. The act of erecting stone was a special event, sometimes accompanied by some kind of deposit, uch as bone, to 'sanctify' it. It involved selecting a stone, digging a pit, ansporting the stone to its site and its erection. Sledges, or rollers and planks, ay have been used for moving the stone, and if the ground was hard with ost the job would have been made easier. Levers and wedges, ropes of hide nd packing stones would have been used to firm the monolith in its pit. The se of a ramp allowed gravity to do some of the work when the stone was tipped to its pit.

ome of the standing stones in the region are cup-marked, which suggests a pecial ritual significance.

THE ASPER'S FIELD STONE

Shap Avenue

Shap means a heap of stones, and at one time "there were several huge stones standing in a row for nearly a mile." (Campden). South of the village are the remains of a granite stone circle, cut by a railway embankment, and there are three stones on private land, known as Goggleby Stone (NY 5592 1509), Aspers Field (NY 5583 1521) and Thunder Stone (NY 552 158). The first two are cup marked and cup and ring marked, and all are scant remains of an avenue of stones.

In south Cumbria, at Kirksanton (SD 1360 8100) is a pair of easily-accessible standing stones, known as **The Giants' Graves,** on the coastal plain with a background of mountains.

MATFEN

THE GIANTS' GRAVES,
Kirksanton (Nr Millom)

Many stone circle and a giant cairn hav been obliterated, what you see is only part of a ritu landscape.

In Northumberlan one of the easie stones to reach, ar most interesting, is **Matfen** (NZ 032 705 On the side of th road opposite th house calle Standing Stone Far (an interestir building) is a larg cup-marked stor that is not in original position.

14

JRIAL MOUNDS

ere are a few long barrows in this region. These early communal Neolithic es were for burial and other rituals that may have been taken over by the nges.

e next development was the round barrow, which at its earliest and most ectacular is best seen in places like Newgrange, Ireland, where a huge und is built over a passageway that leads to stone chambers for the dead.

e most common round barrows are on a much smaller scale, yet varying nsiderably in size, and later in date, often covering the remains of one person, metimes more, and often being reused at a later date. This break away from mmunal burial is mainly an Early Bronze Age feature with the burials metimes accompanied by rich 'grave goods' of flint, metal (gold, copper and onze), beads and pottery.

here there was little stone, the mound could be made by piling the upcast m a circular ditch into the central circular area, over the burial. The body uld lie on the surface, but usually in a pit or in a stone-lined chest (called a st'). The body might be cremated or buried as an inhumation.

indreds of these small mounds, often dug into by treasure hunters of all nturies, survive at least in part, sometimes as crop marks seen from the air, as slight rises in a field or on a moor. They are often marked on maps as mulus', are often difficult to find, and when found, there isn't much to see. wever, there are some fine examples in our region that can be visited.

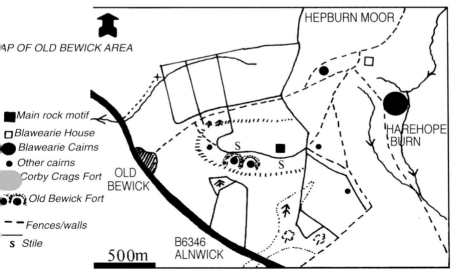

Use the OS Pathfinder 476 map. Access is easiest if you start at Old Bewick Village.

Photograph by Irene Hew

Blawearie (NU 0817 2229)

Old Bewick Moor is private land with well-defined public access. It has attracted not only historians, but has sparked off strong responses from artists and writers. No wonder.

One focus of interest is the reinstated cairn close to Blawearie House, on the public path. Here you can see the depleted ring of stones, about 12m in diameter, that is the kerb of a burial mound. Four cists of different types are open to view in cut-away areas of the platform wall. At the centre, a mound of stones hides a 1.3m deep pit that had an unknown, early ritual purpose. You may see a small kerbed cairn and a tiny circle of stones to the north, all parts of a cemetery of small cairns, not all of them visible.

A slab that now acts as an entrance covers a fragile cist (E) that was the burial place of a cremated woman and child whose bones were mixed with soil and flints before the cover was placed. Cist B, dug in the 1860s contained a flint knife and a necklace of jet and shale beads. Cist A had food vessel. Cist C was empty, and so was the oval, double capped cist D but both may have contained bodies that have disappeared in the acid soil.

You are looking at a site that has long history, and careful excavation what was a very disturbed site brings together what you can see on the ground and what is now in museum or laboratory reports. This sequence helps to bring together what you can and cannot see at the site:

A low sandy knoll was cleared, a kerbed circle tightly built, and an elliptical pit dug at the centre to a depth of 1.3m, lined at the bottom with stones, and then randomly filled in.

The base of a platform wall inside the kerb circle was laid down.

A major change in the use of the cairn began: a series of burials and cremations was inserted beneath the platform wall. Five cists were constructed by disturbing the platform wall and by using uprooted kerbstones to make them. A sixth was built at the centre of the cairn, above the pit. An amber necklace and piece of copper wire ring may have come from one of these cists.

Other rituals were used: a fire pit with hot cremation and burnt flint, a cremation under the platform wall surrounded by small cobbles, and an urn cremation with two adult males.

The site was dug in the 1860's, and during the last war it was used by the army as a foxhole. Despite all this upheaval, it has been possible to extract information of great importance about burial customs around 2,000BC.

Outside the large cairn are two smaller ones, part of a larger cemetery, one of which covered a cremation burial.

Taken from the north-west in 1987, the total excavation area is shown. Stones and soil outside the "cut" have been removed. In the large cairn, the five cists and fire pit show as dark areas. The centre pit is now covered over. To the left, a tarpaulin covers the "little cairn" and its cremation. At the edge, the stones of a tiny, non-burial cairn, have been removed, and wait, lower left, to be replaced.

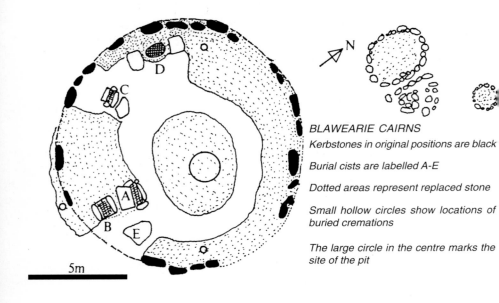

BLAWEARIE CAIRNS

Kerbstones in original positions are black

Burial cists are labelled A-E

Dotted areas represent replaced stone

Small hollow circles show locations of buried cremations

The large circle in the centre marks the site of the pit

5m

Stay in this area for as long as you can, for there is so much to see, including:

1 Two large cup and ring marked rocks, and many others.
2 A hill fort above Corby Crags.
3 Old Bewick double hillfort and a nearby enclosed settlement and cairn.
4 Blawearie House, built in the 1850's, mainly used as a shepherd's house.

Should you want to explore further, there are many cairnfields, including two open cists and a cairn with a standing stone.

Askham Moor: The Moor Divock Cairns

Askham village (NY 515 236) is south-west of Penrith. Askham Fell, which includes Moor Divock, can be reached by public path west out of Askham, or via Helton along an unfenced minor road.

All sites are on paths, and you may see the following:

1 The Copstone standing stone (NY 4960 2160) is set in a faint circle of 21m diameter.

2 A ring cairn (NY 4940 2196) that combines a circle of gapped standing stones with the cairn that they enclose, which, when excavated in the 19th century, contained ashes and broken pottery at the base and a 'food vessel' above. One of the standing stones has a cup and ring mark facing inwards.

3 A burial cairn (NY 4931 2219) which is very disturbed. It had an inverted urn at its centre.

4 This disturbed cairn (NY 4888 2245) has a cist visible at its centre, once containing a contracted skeleton.

5 'The Cockpit' (NY 4827 2224), sometimes described as a ring cairn, sometimes as a stone circle, is a circle of stones containing the remains of a wall, enclosing a large central area. There has been no excavation.

top: RING CAIRN (no. 2 in the text)

There are other cairns and stones, but those described above are close together and easily reached by footpaths.

There is a settlement nearby at Skirsgill Hill (NY 499 233), with 30 acres of field systems and enclosures.

left: THE COPSTONE (no.1 in the text)

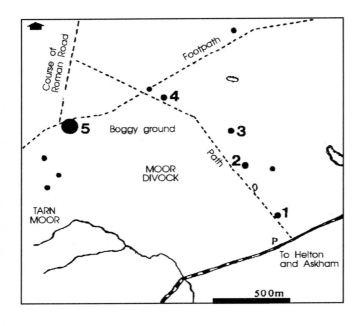

1 The Cop Stone
● 2-4 Burials
   described in text
5 The Cockpit
● Other burial cairns

ROCK MOTIFS

Reference has already been made to markings on stone.

There has been a great upsurge of interest recently in motifs pecked onto rock surfaces with a hard stone pick, a ritual practice that begins in the late Neolithic period from about 3,000BC.

The designs produced are generally called 'cup and ring marks', because a small cup-like depression was commonly pecked into the rock and surrounded with one or more grooves. These designs were not decoration, but were of religious importance to the people who made them; they appear on some standing stones and in burials which suggests a special ritual use.

Why these symbols were chosen in the first place we do not know, but they are quite simple and appear all over the world, without any evidence of contact between people; some symbols and designs seem to belong to many people. Given such basic symbols to start with, it is interesting how many variations they managed to make on the theme.

There are hundreds of rocks marked in this way, recorded in detail, mostly on outcrop rock, but some in a context. The following are recommended because they are accessible and because they are fine examples of Rock Art.

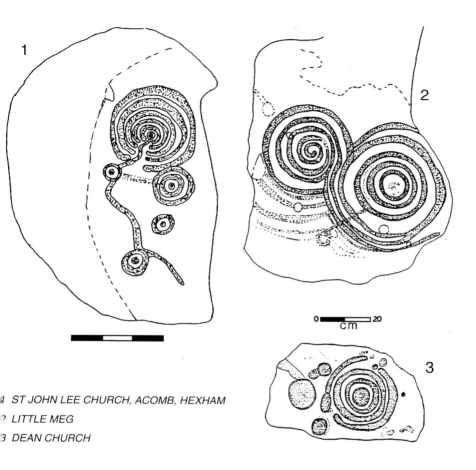

1 *ST JOHN LEE CHURCH, ACOMB, HEXHAM*

2 *LITTLE MEG*

3 *DEAN CHURCH*

Roughting Linn (NT 983 376) has the largest spread of outcrop rock motifs in northern England. Known for over 150 years, and still unsignposted, it is hidden from the road by bushes, but it is easily accessible. Turn west off the B6525 road from Doddington to Berwick at a blue and white bungalow. After about two miles, a wood on either side of this minor road and a sign to Roughting Linn farm show that you are in the right area. The rock is north, a few metres from the road through a gap in the bushes (north-east of the farm road).

There is also a very good 'promontory' Iron Age fort at the site, and a path to the waterfall and pond that gives the site its name: a pond in which the water bellows.

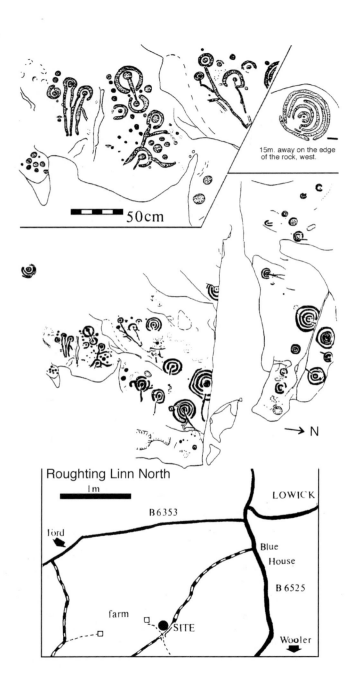

15m. away on the edge of the rock, west.

50cm

Roughting Linn North

1 m

→ N

LOWICK

B 6353

ford

Blue
House

B 6525

farm

SITE

Wooler

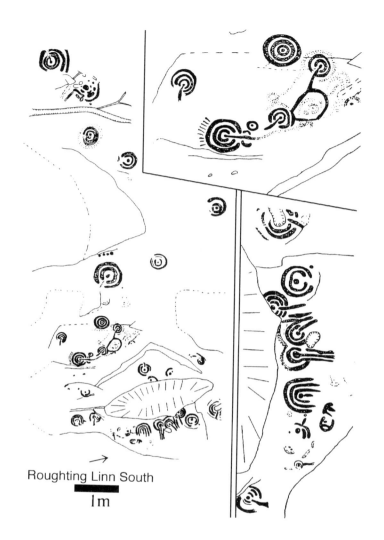

Roughting Linn South

1 m

Photograph by Ian Hewitt

Below are three examples of Old Bewick rock motifs.

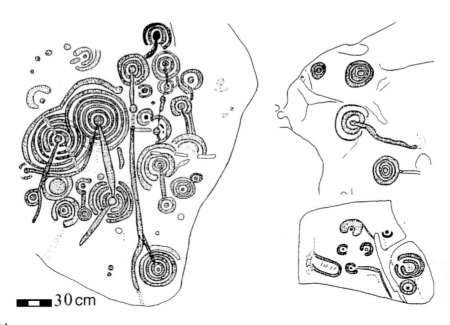

30 cm

Lordenshaw (NZ 054 992)

This small selection is easily accessible. The importance of Rock Art sites is that they show a wide distribution across the landscape, and may mark routeways, territorial divisions and 'special' places, particularly for nomadic people. None of Cumbria's markings is on outcrop rock, whereas most of Northumberland's are.

1 m

Above is the main rock, west of the fort, partly quarried away and vandalised. Below is the 'Horseshoe Rock', located by following a field wall downhill, north west. Both stand on ridges that have extensive views.

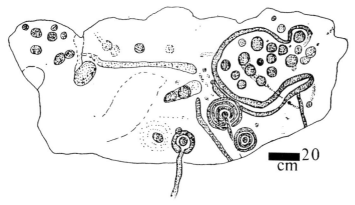

20 cm

SETTLEMENTS AND DEFENCES

This section concentrates on the Iron Age period, although some sites continue to be used in Roman times.

So far we have looked at ceremonial sites. Sites where people lived and worked are often buried; some have been excavated and covered over again. Some can still be seen, especially when the sun is low in the sky, when deep shadows are thrown by walls and ditches, by the trackways leading to them, and by field walls. Looking for such sites is a most interesting way of spending time in the open air, especially in the winter. Traces are slight because houses were built of wood and thatch, fences erected on low walls fall down and decay when a settlement is abandoned and fields become reused or abandoned. As hunting and herding were always important, and as arable land can deteriorate through being over-used, many settlements may have been very temporary, where easily-constructed tents and huts would have sufficed, and leave hardly a trace. It is sometimes difficult to find a single hut site on a platform on a hillside. There is much more chance of seeing an enclosure wall and ditch that surround a group of hut circles, especially if the huts have stone foundations. Out in the field, as opposed to being up in the air, you are most likely to see sites that are on high ground, on land that no one has wanted to cultivate since prehistoric times. Lower sites are more likely to appear as crop marks.

Many enclosed and unenclosed settlements are known in the region, along with traces of ancient fields that served them, but the most prominent enclosures tend to be hillforts,

strongly built to resist attack. They may, as has been proved by excavation, lie on top of earlier settlements that can't be seen. A good site can attract people for centuries.

Fortifications can be built to keep out wild animals, but mostly they are built to keep out other people. It seems that life was a struggle to use nature to advantage, to cope with crop failures, disease and other ills, without fighting each other, but fight they did, especially when there were shortages. The number of hillforts in this region, belonging to the Late Bronze and Early Iron Ages, speaks of tribalism, of setting up defences, saying, "This is my patch - keep off!" We can't calculate how many people there were at any given time, or know how many of the defensive enclosures were in use at one time, or whether a particular fort, was ever attacked, without thorough excavation - and that is impossible, given the expense of modern archaeology and its priority in our national budget. It is highly unlikely that a regional group of people could live in a hillfort all the time, even though they might all have had a hand in building it. We have to make use of what information there is from the better excavated sites, along with accurate recording on the ground, to make sense of what we see. Even so, other regional 'models' may not necessarily apply to this area.

The principles of all enclosures, though, are similar: enclose an area by digging a ditch, and use the upcast to make a wall. This wall could be faced with quarried stone, and have a palisade (fence) built on top. It would need a strong gate. Extra defences

CORBY CRAGS, BLAWEARIE, HILLFORT

could be added by digging more ditches and building more walls outside or inside the original one. Inside would be some huts, circular arrangements a bit like wigwams, later with a narrow stone wall to support the timbers, and a thatched roof. People on the walls defended the settlement by hurling or firing objects at attackers, before the hand to hand fighting. Gates were sometimes burnt or battered down, and particular attention was paid to defending them.

These defences varied considerably in size. Yeavering Bell, in Northumberland, is the largest, with over 130 hut circles inside it, though how anyone could actually live up there is difficult to understand as it can be very cold even in summer! Some 'forts' have traces of only one or two huts. It was in some such stockades that people prepared to defend themselves against the Romans, having used them previously to warn off their neighbours.

The defended sites may have replaced lightly-defended or undefended enclosures, but they provided a focus for the people living in the area. It is in the field systems, where ploughing, sowing and gathering took place, in the woods where pigs and deer roamed, in pasture where sheep, cattle and goats were grazed and the rivers and lakes that people made their living and established their small farms. Their traces may be seen as hillside terraces (lynchets), the faint combed pattern of 'cord rig' ploughing and faint field walls. The remains of their pottery and tools may be scattered in modern ploughsoil where the land is still worth ploughing, or stored in museums and other collections. Wealth was always land principally. Gold, amber, imported and local luxury goods had to be paid for through surplus production or the concentration of wealth in the hands of a few, the reward for being born with the right status, strength or cunning. The essentials were food and shelter, and with this security people could develop their relationships, have children, think their thoughts, and wonder what lay beyond all that. The search for people is elusive, so we have to assume that the basic needs are what link them to us. They had different knowledge, skills and technology, but must have been like us in so many ways But we can only guess and speculate.

Some people may have specialised because they could trade a skill. There may have been some division of labour within a group where someone excelled in pottery, ornaments or fine tools. One group, living close to sources of ore, might have excelled in metallurgy. Good hunters may have been able to barter rare animal skins. Perhaps the storyteller, the singer, the person with a good memory, was much in demand and enjoyed high status for such skills. We don't know how much everyone was expected to be good at everything! We see through a glass darkly; it is rare that we come face to face with 'real' people. Their bones tell us something: height, age, sex, health and sometimes the cause of death, but not really very much about them.

OLD BEWICK DOUBLE HILLFORT

The **Ingram Valley** is one of the most important Prehistoric Sites in Britain. The 'fossilized' field systems of Prehistoric and Medieval times show that the area was able to support crops in places where there is now only grazing and forestry. To fly over it in strong, low sunshine reveals a dense pattern of such fields and settlements that have recently begun to be recorded thoroughly.

In the Cheviots, generally, small piles of stones mark field clearance and not burial, from about 2,000BC onward. Unenclosed hut sites are visible to the practised eye, but what stands out are enclosures and huts that have stone bases for walls that were made of timber. Some of these settlements had their timber palisades replaced by more substantial stone fortification. Brough Law is a good example of a stone fort. (NT 998 164)

The name 'Brough', as in 'burgh' and 'bury', means fortification. Its stone walls were erected about 2,200 years ago. A walk from the car park to the top passes smaller enclosures, a more recent farm enclosure, and rig and furrow ploughing. The view from the top shows why the fort was built there: there is a sheer drop to the valley. Its double rampart is made of stone rubble inside a stone skin. The entrance is at the east, where there used to be a timber gateway, but as you walk around the ramparts you see how the outer rampart merges with the inner: the steep slope did not require any more strength, whereas the gateway needed defence in depth. Its date from excavation makes it pre-Roman, but it may have been used afterwards.

The site is only one of many excellent examples in the same area, and National Parks is studying ways of making even more parts of it accessible to the public.

BROUGH LAW HILLFORT FROM THE WEST
The path from the car park appears by the wood at the top left of the picture.

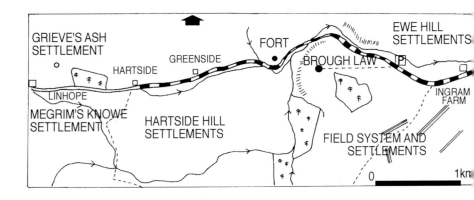

LORDENSHAW FROM THE NORTH-WEST

1 Site of recent shieling
2 Hollow way
3 Incomplete defensive earthwork
4 Faint outer earthwork
5 Outer ditch and counterscarp
6 Hollow trackway, to east entrance

7 Late enclosure and settlement of round houses (Romano-British)
8 Inner rampart, possibly late
9 Large stone-based hut circle
10 East entrance
Between 5 and 8 is a faint, inner ditch

Lordenshaw (NZ 0545 9925)

A recent management agreement between National Parks and the Duke of Northumberland has made this interesting, multi-phase area accessible to the public. A starting point for exploration is a large, new car park just off the Hexham - Rothbury road.

The hill fort is a focal point. Although it has its origin in the Iron Age, or earlier, a small settlement of Romano-British round houses has been built inside, and in an enclosure that breaks up part of the earlier ramparts and ditches.

There is an extra rampart to the west that is not continued to the east, and the area that it seems intended to enclose was a large one, possibly for stock.

There are two entrances, and the eastern one is linked to an impressive hollow way, well-defined with standing and other stones.

Lordenshaw is not the highest part of the Simonside Hills, but it has dominant views and is a focus of routes from the Whitton Burn and River Coquet.

The earliest evidence of people there is on the rocks: motifs have been pecked on to them and some cairns constructed on them. One cairn has not only been raised on cup-marked outcrop, but two of its kerbs have cups. All the cairns have been dug, one has two cists inside and another has two cup-marked boulders in its destroyed centre.

The area has been used constantly since then; you can see a medieval deer park pale, shielings, hollow ways, quarries and rig and furrow ploughing of different periods.

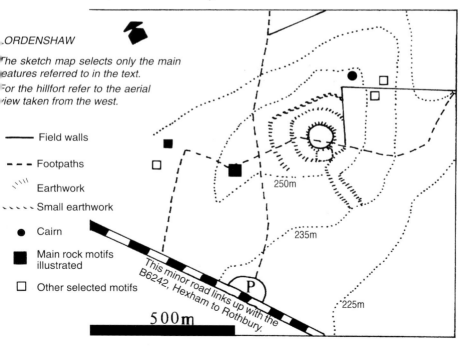

LORDENSHAW

The sketch map selects only the main features referred to in the text.
For the hillfort refer to the aerial view taken from the west.

——— Field walls

- - - Footpaths

Earthwork

Small earthwork

● Cairn

■ Main rock motifs illustrated

□ Other selected motifs

This minor road links up with the B6242, Hexham to Rothbury.

500m

250m

235m

225m

P

Carrock Fell Hillfort, Cumbria (OS sheet 90 NY 343 337)

Carrock Fell (rock fell) is the eastern edge of the Skiddaw massif. North of the A66 road betwee *Penrith and Keswick, a minor road runs to Mungrisdale (pig's valley where St. Mungo's churc* *stood) and Mosedale (valley with a peat bog), beyond which, west of an unfenced road, the cli* *face of Carrock Fell rises from the valley of the River Caldew (cold river) as it makes a sharp tur* *north. Look out for Stone Ends farm, due east of the fell and road.*

There is parking space among the boulders, by a long, narrow quarry.

There are many unsignposted paths leading west to the summit, all steep and difficult. Keep a sma *stream to your left, and aim at a rowan tree that stands on a prominent outcrop, via the scree. Nea* *the top, the paths reach a wider path from Mosedale that leads first to a stone shelter and cairn o* *the way north-west to the summit. It is a tough climb, and alternatives from Mosedale are als* *difficult, so good footwear, good weather and care are essential. Once at the top, the effort i* *worthwhile, with some of the finest views from any British hillfort.*

PART OF THE HILLFORT WALL

At 700m (2,150'), the walls are constructed as a contour fort enclosing 5 acres with a prominent outcrop to the west giving way to a series of boulder strew and grassed sloping platforms that get lower to the east and end with a cli face. The interest is in the scale of its construction and its dominant position. has not been excavated, so nothing can be said about it, except that no on could live in it for most of the year. It is a focal, defensive point that could hav had a history reaching into the Bronze Age, typical of hillforts that preceded th arrival of the Romans, whose camps are to be seen guarding the lines o communication on lower ground.

A large cairn with its centre removed, now used as a shelter for hikers, stand inside the fort, and is probably Bronze Age.